French Kitchenware

Monique Cabré

L'Aventurine

Contents

Appetizers 5
Cutting 6
Crushing 14
Cracking 16
Grating 18
Grinding 20
Refining 22
Cooking 26
Grilling 36
Frying 38
Transporting 40
Preserving 42
Decorating 48
Serving 56
Presenting 62
Uncorking 66
Pouring 70
Drinking 78
Draining 82
Organizing 86
Wiping 92

Translation: William Wheeler
Photographs: Robert Canault.

ISBN 2-84190-042-8

Appetizers

Salt-glazed earthenware honey pot.
Beauvaisis, 1840.

Once upon a time, the French kitchen was a wonderful place filled with utensils as beautiful as they were useful. That was the time when each household prepared its own bread, butter and cheese and each utensil had a well-defined role to play.

Whether they be in ceramics, metal, wood or glass, these objects are steeped in tradition. They have accompanied generations of housekeepers in their daily culinary tasks. Some of them are basic and rudimentary while others contain ingenious mechanisms.

Every region of France was fiercely individualistic and folk art accordingly reflects the specific origins of peasants and craftsmen. The beauty and functionality of the kitchen utensils they produced command our respect and represent an invaluable contribution to France's artistic heritage. These objects however also strike a common emotional chord which, by its very nature, can be felt by many people everywhere.

Antique kitchenware reminds us of a time when life followed the rhythm of the seasons and time advanced at a horse's pace. Traditions were respected. Able craftsmen produced handsome, quality wares, so much so that centuries later we still admire them for their beauty and elegance. Glazed earthenware, carved wood, wrought iron, copper and blown glass were chosen as materials for their sturdiness and intrinsic value. Seen through the veil of the past, they also take on that intangible quality of nostalgia.

As you turn the pages of this book, you will discover how life used to be in a French kitchen: copper molds, butter stamps, preserving jars, coffee grinders, enamel coffee pots, all as they were in times past.

Stoneware vinegar crock.
Alsace, 1741.

Iron cleaver.
19th century.

Cutting

Iron cleaver with wooden handle. 19th century.

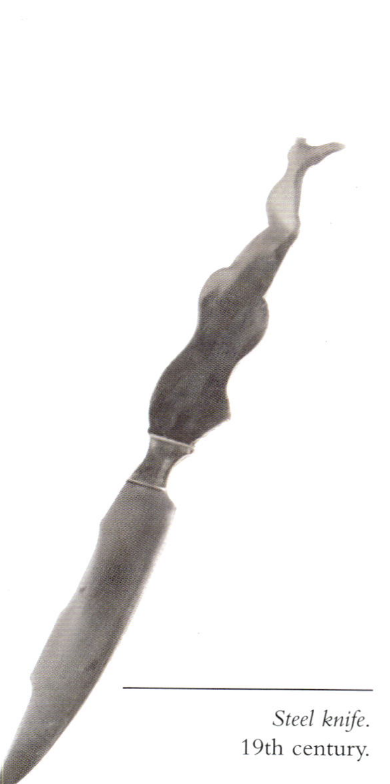

Steel knife.
19th century.

A knife is a piece of metal composed of a sharpened blade and its continuation, the tang, covered by a protective handle. The latter can be in wood, metal, horn or in porcelain.

Prior to the late 16th century when matching sets were first produced, knives were unique objects used as multi-purpose tools as well as to stab pieces of meat and poultry at the dinner table.

Once meat had been cut into smaller pieces with knives or cleavers, it could then be minced with different types of choppers, with single or multiple steel or wrought iron blades. They had wooden handles or, in the case of curved blade choppers, wooden grasps at both ends.

Wood and wrought iron fox-shaped cleaver. 19th century.

Steel chopper with wooden grips. 19th century.

Steel fox-shaped cleaver. 19th century.

Steel chopper with five blades. 19th century.

Iron horse-shaped cleaver with wooden handle. 19th century.

Iron cleaver with turned boxwood handle. 19th century.

Venery scissors. 19th century.

Pocket knives with a silver blade for cheese and a steel blade for fruit. 18th century.

Matching iron knife and cleaver with linoleum handles. 19th century.

Opinel pocket knives. Early 20th century.

Kitchen knives.
Early 20th century.

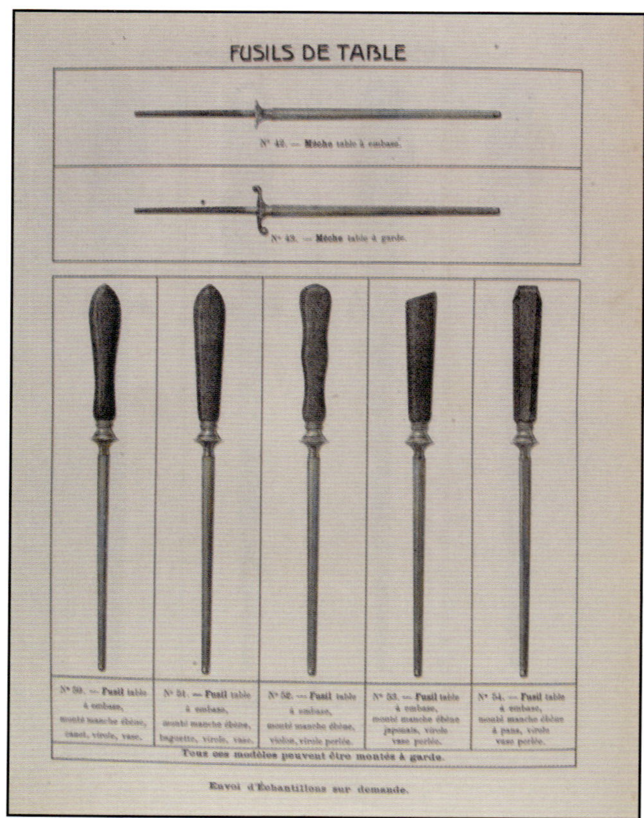

FUSILS DE TABLE

N° 48. — **Mèche** table à embase.

N° 49. — **Mèche** table à garde.

N° 50. — **Fusil** table à embase, monté manche ébène, canel, virole, vase.	N° 51. — **Fusil** table à embase, monté manche ébène, baguette, virole, vase.	N° 52. — **Fusil** table à embase, monté manche ébène, violon, virole perlée.	N° 53. — **Fusil** table à embase, monté manche ébène japonais, virole vase perlée.	N° 54. — **Fusil** table à embase, monté manche ébène à pans, virole vase perlée.

Tous ces modèles peuvent être montés à garde.

Envoi d'Échantillons sur demande.

Whetstone with turned wooden handle and chain. 19th century.

Whetstone with brass handle. 19th century.

Pages from *Album des fusils de bouchers et de table,* Rameau cutlery works. 1902.

Whetstone with turned wooden handle. 19th century.

Whetstone with staghorn handle. 19th century.

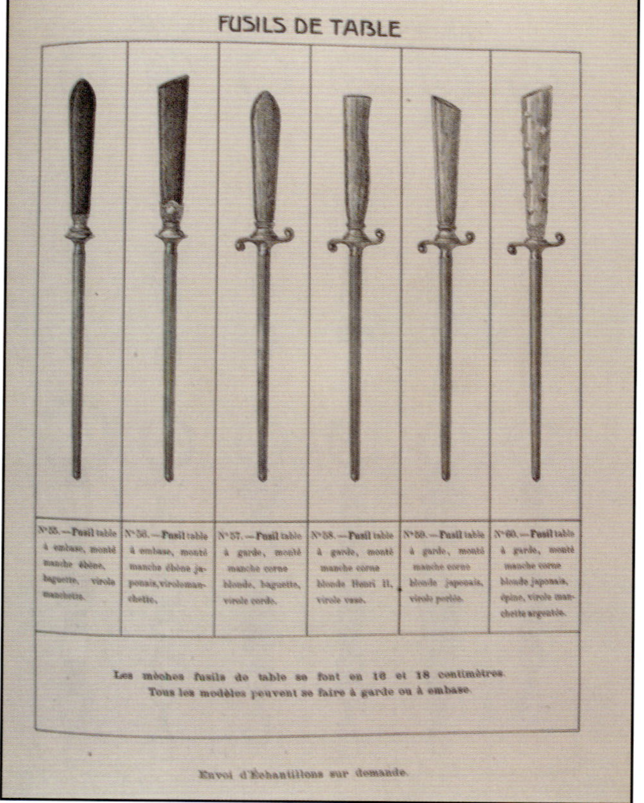

FUSILS DE TABLE

N° 55. — **Fusil** table à embase, monté manche ébène, baguette, virole manchette.	N° 56. — **Fusil** table à embase, monté manche ébène japonais, virole manchette.	N° 57. — **Fusil** table à garde, monté manche corne blonde, baguette, virole corde.	N° 58. — **Fusil** table à garde, monté manche corne blonde Henri II, virole vase.	N° 59. — **Fusil** table à garde, monté manche corne blonde japonais, virole perlée.	N° 60. — **Fusil** table à garde, monté manche corne blonde japonais, épine, virole manchette argentée.

Les mèches fusils de table se font en 16 et 18 centimètres.
Tous les modèles peuvent se faire à garde ou à embase.

Envoi d'Échantillons sur demande.

Kitchen knives.
19th and 20th centuries.

Bread cutting boards with knives or cleavers.
19th century.

Chocolate cutter.
19th century.

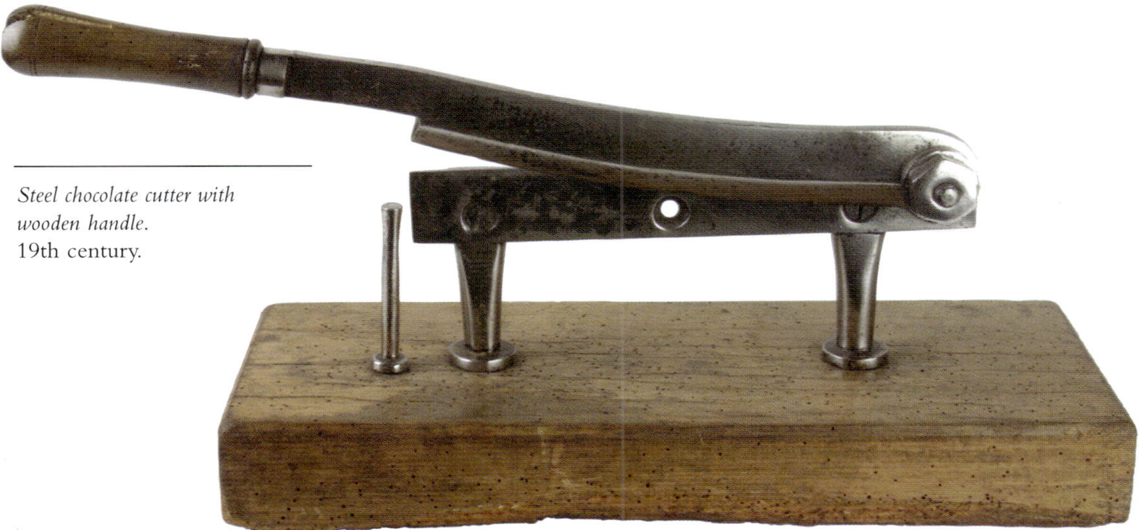

Steel chocolate cutter with wooden handle.
19th century.

Crushing

Wooden mortar and pestle. Early 19th century.

Porcelain mortar and pestle. Early 20th century.

Walnut mortar and pestle. 19th century.

Olivewood mortar with porcelain pestle. Provence, 19th century.

Turned wood mortar and pestle. Early 20th century.

A basic kitchen utensil used around the world, the mortar crushes ingredients, reduces them to a powder or mashes them to a purée. It was essential when preparing spice mixtures or certain traditional sauces and soups, such as *aïoli,* a garlic-based mayonnaise from Provence or *pistou,* a vegetable soup with crushed basil from Marseille and Nice.

Because they did not absorb the odors of crushed ingredients, only the hardest and smoothest unporous materials such as marble and porcelain were suitable for mortars. Mortars were also produced in hardwoods, stoneware, cast iron and stone but these were best employed with dry mixtures. The same requirements held true for pestles.

Stoneware mortar with wooden pestle. Bresse, 1881.

Walnut and boxwood pestles.
19th century.

Double wooden pestle.
Late 19th century.

Limestone mortar.
19th century.

Cast-iron mortar.
17th century.

Glazed earthenware mortar with wooden pestle.
Late 19th century.

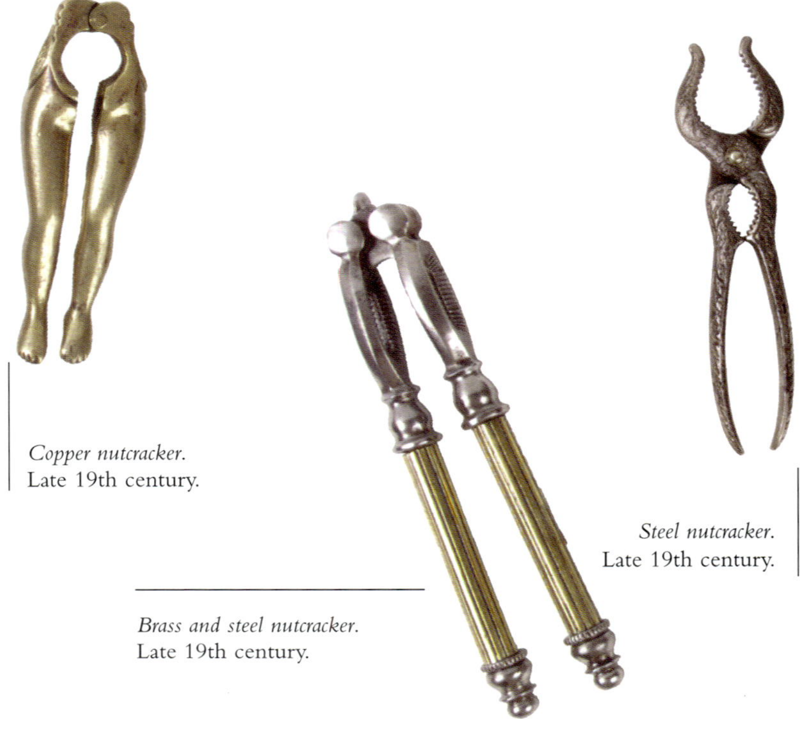

Copper nutcracker.
Late 19th century.

Steel nutcracker.
Late 19th century.

Brass and steel nutcracker.
Late 19th century.

Carved wood nutcracker.
First half of 19th century.

Cracking

True to their name, nutcrackers are used to break open the shells of edible nuts, principally walnuts and hazel nuts, without crushing the meat, an advantage over hammers and mallets. Nutcrackers are based on a very simple principle: two metal stems, most often in steel, brass, or wrought iron are joined by a hinge. It is so elementary that craftsmen could easily express their creative skills, imagining models decorated with flowers and animals, arabesques and scrolls, resembling bird's beaks or sneering human faces.
Some nutcrackers function like presses: as the screw is tightened, the nut is squeezed until it bursts. Cage nutcrackers, some elaborately carved in wood, use the same system.

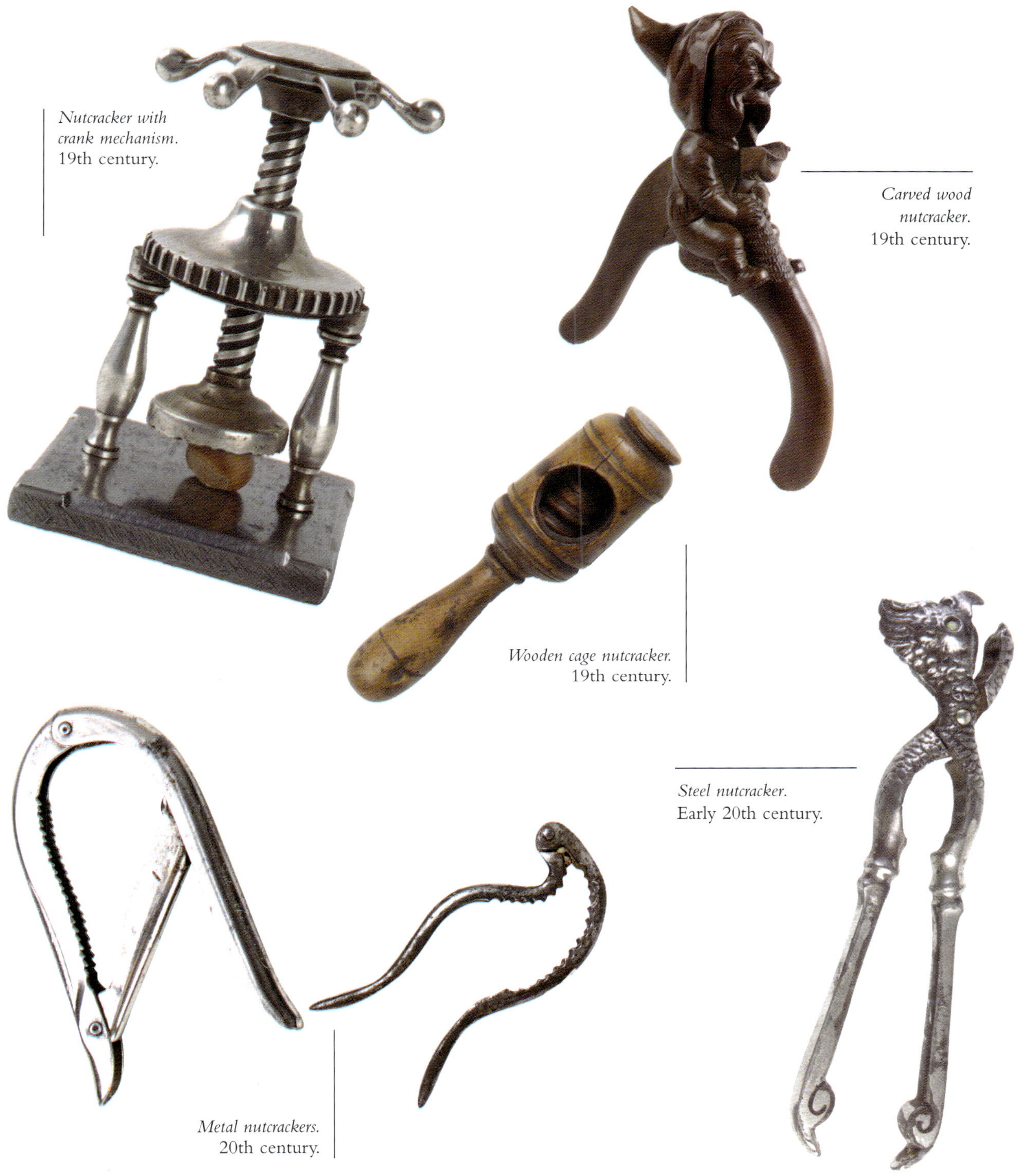

Nutcracker with crank mechanism.
19th century.

Carved wood nutcracker.
19th century.

Wooden cage nutcracker.
19th century.

Steel nutcracker.
Early 20th century.

Metal nutcrackers.
20th century.

Grating

Iron grater.
20th century.

Iron grater with walnut frame.
Provence, 19th century.

Iron grater.
20th century.

Graters reduce solid food into filaments or a powder by rubbing it against a metal plate covered with raised jagged edges. The size and position of the perforations depended on the exact use of the grater, although sometimes they were arranged in essentially decorative patterns. For easy and efficient use, graters were equipped with solid handles or mounted on wooden panels; some featured storage compartments. There were models for grating cheese, bread, chocolate or nutmeg, and still others for vegetables. Hand graters were first supplanted by mechanical vegetable shredders with interchangeable blades, and then again more recently by electric blenders.

Iron and beechwood cabbage grater. Alsace, 19th century.

Iron grater with wooden frame. 19th century.

Nutmeg grater with storage compartment. 19th century.

Iron grater. 19th century.

Iron grater with storage compartment. 20th century.

Painted metal and wood Peugeot Frères coffee grinders. 20th century.

Grinding

Metal coffee grinder. 20th century.

Coffee mills of all shapes and sizes, be they round or square, table or wall models, inevitably evoke daily traditional family life. History has it that Louis XIV drank his first swallow of coffee in 1644. At the end of the 17th century, the first small machines for grinding roasted coffee beans were produced for home use.

The basic coffee mill would undergo several modifications: one model, familiarly called the Louis XIV, could be fastened to the table, while others with larger storage capacities were attached to the wall. They were carved in wild cherry or produced in iron, engraved copper or silver, or inlaid with mother of pearl. During the 18th century, as production levels increased, less precious materials were employed. Starting in the 1870's, manufacturers such as Peugeot, Japy or Goldenberg presented numerous models of coffee mills in their catalogues, constantly updated, which slowly but surely replaced machines produced by local craftsmen in smaller series.

Metal and wood coffee grinder. 20th century.

Painted metal and wood Peugeot Frères coffee grinder. 20th century.

Wood and copper coffee grinder. Late 19th century.

Painted metal and wood coffee Peugeot Frères grinder. 20th century.

Painted metal and wood Grand-mère coffee grinder. 20th century.

Painted metal and wood Sanpeur coffee grinder. 20th century.

Refining

Wooden butter churn.
19th century.

Stoneware butter churn with wooden plunger.
19th century.

The making of cream, butter and cheese from cow, goat and ewe milk permits the conservation of these highly perishable raw products for longer periods of time. Fresh milk left in basins for twenty-four hours in a cool room separates with the fat content rising to the top. This cream was poured off or skimmed off with a wooden cream ladle. Making butter required more energy, because cream must be churned or agitated. Cream was poured into the churn, a cylindrical wooden container, then agitated with a plunger until butter formed. It was then washed and worked to make it smooth and unctuous. To make farmer's cheese, milk was left to curdle by natural bacterial action. It was then slowly drained in special slotted metal, porcelain, glazed earthenware, or wicker molds.

Glazed earthenware cheese mold. 19th century.

Glazed earthenware cheese mold. Late 19th century.

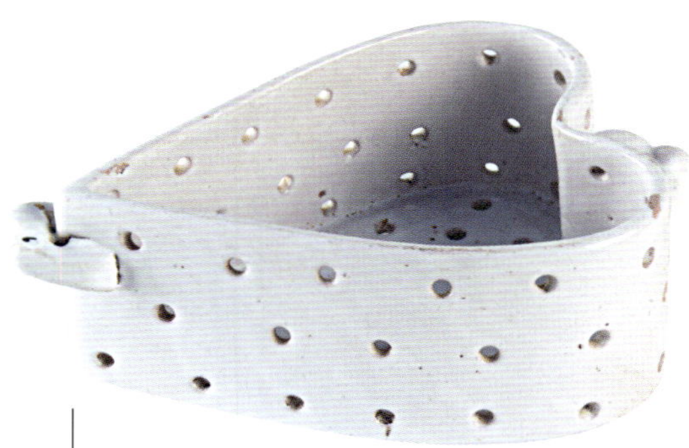

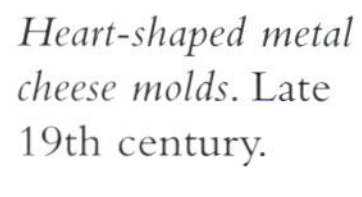

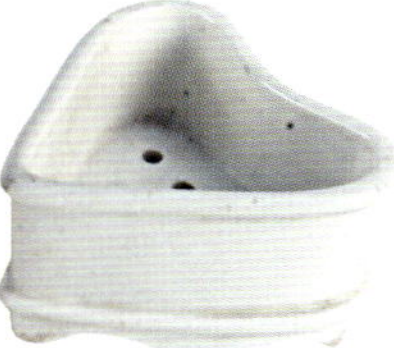

Heart-shaped metal cheese molds. Late 19th century.

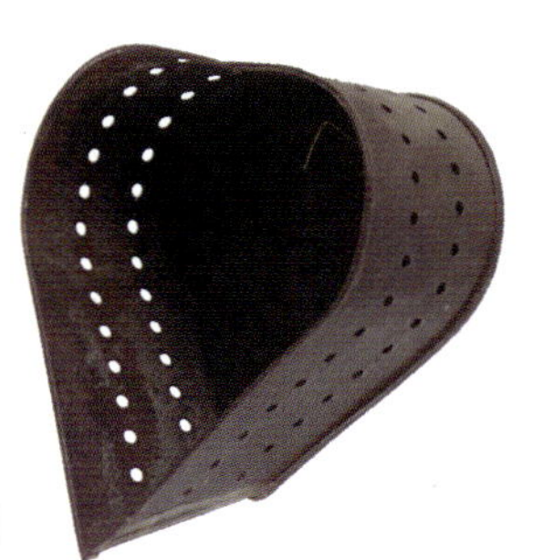

Heart-shaped porcelain cheese molds. Late 19th century.

Cheese molds

Often produced in glazed earthenware, but also in wicker or metal, cheese molds were very common objects in kitchens. Lined with muslin, they were filled with milk curd and left to drain slowly. Traditional forms for these molds varied from region to region. In the Center, they were rectangular; in the Sarthe, tall and cylindrical; in the Dordogne, tripod molds were decorated with a brownish glaze. In the Cher, farmer's cheese was prepared in round orange-glazed basins.

Metal beater with wooden handle. 20th century.

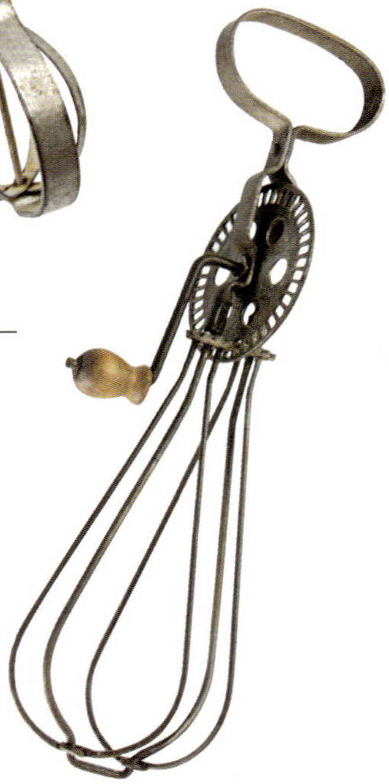

Metal beaters. First half of 20th century.

Whisk with wooden handle. Early 20th century.

Whisks

For centuries, eggs were beaten with a little whisk made from birch or willow twigs. A wooden spatula was traditionally used to beat egg whites. At the end of the 18th century, the first simple wire whisks were produced.

Mayonnaise beaters.
20th century.

Mayonnaise beaters

Making mayonnaise takes a certain culinary know-how. Using a specially designed beater could facilitate the process. A mechanical beater was attached to the cover of a glass jar; more sophisticated models also featured an adjustable funnel. The beater was held in one hand by the handle while the other grasped the jar. The *nec plus ultra* of these machines could be connected directly to the sink tap and the beater was activated by water power. It took approximately 40 liters of water to make a jar of mayonnaise.

Glazed earthenware cooking pot.
Beauvaisis, 19th century.

Cooking

Three-footed glazed earthenware tart cooker.
Jura, 19th century.

Glazed earthenware tripe pot. Late 19th century.

Until a fairly recent time in rural areas, most of the food was cooked in the fireplace. Most often in glazed earthenware, cooking pots filled with meat and vegetables to be braised or boiled were placed directly on top of embers in the hearth. These same embers served to heat small ovens.

The first cast-iron stoves in 1830 and later followed by the innovative gas stoves in 1850 changed life in the kitchen. This more concentrated source of heat contributed to a generalization of the use of metal pots and pans.

Three-footed glazed earthenware stewing pan. Early 20th century.

Three-footed cast-iron stewing pan. Early 20th century.

Copper stewing pan. 19th century.

Stewing pans

Stewing pans were used to simmer certain fat or tough pieces of meat. This type of cooking was characterized by a source of heat coming from above as well as below the pan. They featured recessed fitted lids which were covered with glowing embers or hot water. Placed directly on the hearth, they acted as small portable ovens. These pans were traditionally produced in glazed earthenware, cast iron, or copper. Some models were equipped with feet.

Copper jambonnière.
19th century.

Everything but the oink!

Every winter, the killing of the hog marked a high point in peasant life. It was a festive time when families worked together. The men slaughtered and cut up the animal, while the women organized the cooking and the preparation of even the cheapest cuts. Nothing was wasted. There were different types of sausages to make: *boudin* - traditional blood sausage - or fresh *saucisse*. There were also the loins to prepare, as well as bacon and the large *saucisson sec* sausage to cure. But the ham was the pièce de résistance. It was cooked in a specially-adapted pan called the *jambonnière* whose shape is more or less that of a ham. Depending on the region, it was produced in glazed earthenware, enamel or copper. Of an imposing size, the *jambonnière* featured two sturdy handles and a heavy lid. Some models which were placed directly on the hearth had feet.

Three footed copper dripping pan. Late 19th century.

Glazed earthenware dripping pans. Late 19th century.

Dripping pans

Placed under the grill or the spit, the dripping pan caught meat juices and fat. They were usually made of glazed earthenware and were equipped with handles, pouring spouts and sometimes feet.

Glazed earthenware casserole dishes. 19th century. These models were used for woodcock *pâté*.

Glazed earthenware casserole dishes. Early 20th century.

Casserole dishes

Casserole dishes could be in all sizes and shapes - round, oval, rectangular or oblong - but they all had covers. They were all-purpose because they were not only used as cooking vessels (in a slow oven or a *bain-marie*), but they served also as molds and serving dishes. In traditional French cooking, casserole dishes or *terrines* were used to prepare meat and game *pâtés*. Covers were sometimes decorated with representations of the main ingredient of the *pâté*.

Glazed earthenware casserole dish. Early 20th century.

Glazed earthenware casserole dish. Champagne, 18th century. This model was used for hare *pâté*.

Matching copper sauce pans. Early 20th century.

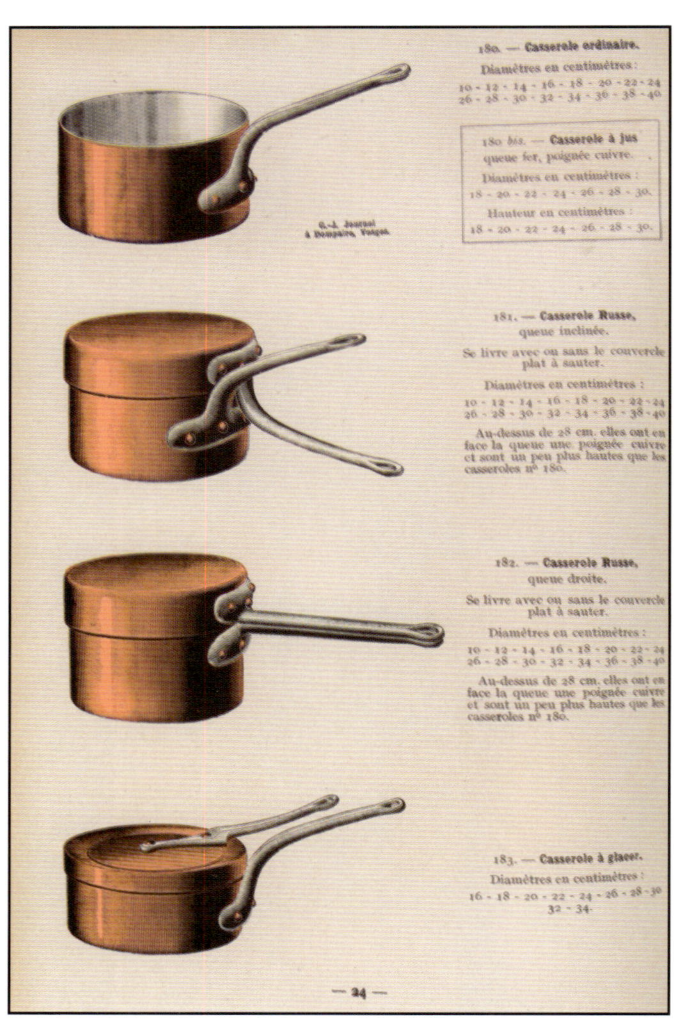

G.-J. Journel
à Dompaire, Vosges

180. — **Casserole ordinaire.**

Diamètres en centimètres :

10 - 12 - 14 - 16 - 18 - 20 - 22 - 24
26 - 28 - 30 - 32 - 34 - 36 - 38 - 40

180 *bis.* — **Casserole à jus**

queue fer, poignée cuivre.

Diamètres en centimètres :

18 - 20 - 22 - 24 - 26 - 28 - 30.

Hauteur en centimètres :

18 - 20 - 22 - 24 - 26 - 28 - 30.

181. — **Casserole Russe,**

queue inclinée.

Se livre avec ou sans le couvercle plat à sauter.

Diamètres en centimètres :

10 - 12 - 14 - 16 - 18 - 20 - 22 - 24
26 - 28 - 30 - 32 - 34 - 36 - 38 - 40

Au-dessus de 28 cm. elles ont en face la queue une poignée cuivre et sont un peu plus hautes que les casseroles nº 180.

182. — **Casserole Russe,**

queue droite.

Se livre avec ou sans le couvercle plat à sauter.

Diamètres en centimètres :

10 - 12 - 14 - 16 - 18 - 20 - 22 - 24
26 - 28 - 30 - 32 - 34 - 36 - 38 - 40

Au-dessus de 28 cm. elles ont en face la queue une poignée cuivre et sont un peu plus hautes que les casseroles nº 180.

183. — **Casserole à glacer.**

Diamètres en centimètres :

16 - 18 - 20 - 22 - 24 - 26 - 28 - 30
32 - 34.

— 24 —

Page from *Catalogue de fournitures générales de cuisine,* G. J. Journel Co. Early 20th century.

Saucepans

Cylindrical vessels with a handle and a lid, saucepans have been in use since the 14th century. However, production levels remained low until the early 18th century and it was only during the following century that saucepans became indispensable to the well-equipped French kitchen at the same time that classic French kitchen utensils became codified. Copper saucepans were preferred because of their sturdiness, despite the time and effort necessary for regular upkeep - without which the metal surfaces reacted with the ingredients and became poisonous! Copper pans are highly sought-after collector's items; their thickness is a good indication of age.

Copper lids with iron handles.
Early 20th century.

197. — **Couvercle à degré,** queue fer.

198. — **Couvercle à degré,** poignée cuivre.

199. — **Couvercle plat,** queue fer.

Diamètres en centimètres : 10-11-12-13-14-15-16-17-18-19-20-21-22-23-24-25-26-27-28-29-30-31-32-33-34-35-36-37-38-39-40-41-42-43-44-45-46-48-50.

G.-J. Journel à Dompaire, Vosges.

200. — **Jambonnière.** Longueurs en centimètres : 40-45-50-55-60.

201. — **Boîte à asperges.** Longueurs en centimètres : 24-26-28-30-32-34-36-38-40-45-50-55.

202. **Marabout** cuivre étamé. Contenance en litres : *1l, 2l, 3l, 4l, 5l, 6l, 7l, 8l, 9l, 10 litres.*

203. **Bouilloire** cuivre. Contenance en litres : *1l, 2l, 3l, 4l, 5l, 6l, 7l, 8l, 9l, 10 litres.*

— 27 —

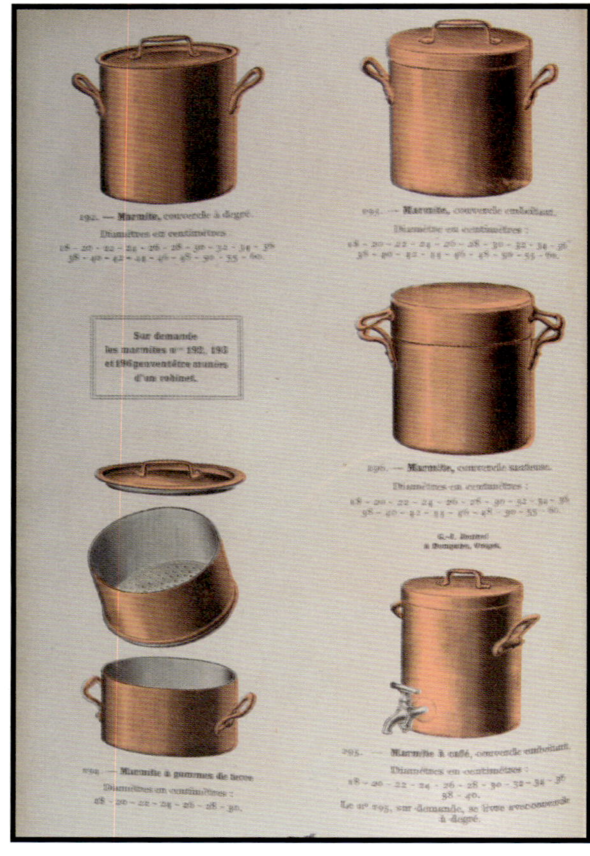

192. — **Marmite,** couvercle à degré.
Diamètres en centimètres :
18-20-22-24-26-28-30-32-34-36-38-40-42-44-46-48-50-55-60.

[illegible]. — **Marmite,** couvercle emboîtant.
Diamètres en centimètres :
18-20-22-24-26-28-30-32-34-36-38-40-42-44-46-48-50-55-60.

Sur demande les marmites nos 192, 193 et 196 peuvent être munies d'un robinet.

196. — **Marmite,** couvercle [illegible].
Diamètres en centimètres :
18-20-22-24-26-28-30-32-34-36-38-40-42-44-46-48-50-55-60.

G.-J. Journel à Dompaire, Vosges.

194. — **Marmite à pommes de terre.**
Diamètres en centimètres :
18-20-22-24-26-28-30.

195. — **Marmite à café,** couvercle emboîtant.
Diamètres en centimètres :
18-20-22-24-26-28-30-32-34-36-38-40.
Le no 195, sur demande, se livre avec couvercle à degré.

Pages from *Catalogue de fournitures générales de cuisine,* G. J. Journel Co. Early 20th century.

Copper braising pans.
Early 20th century.

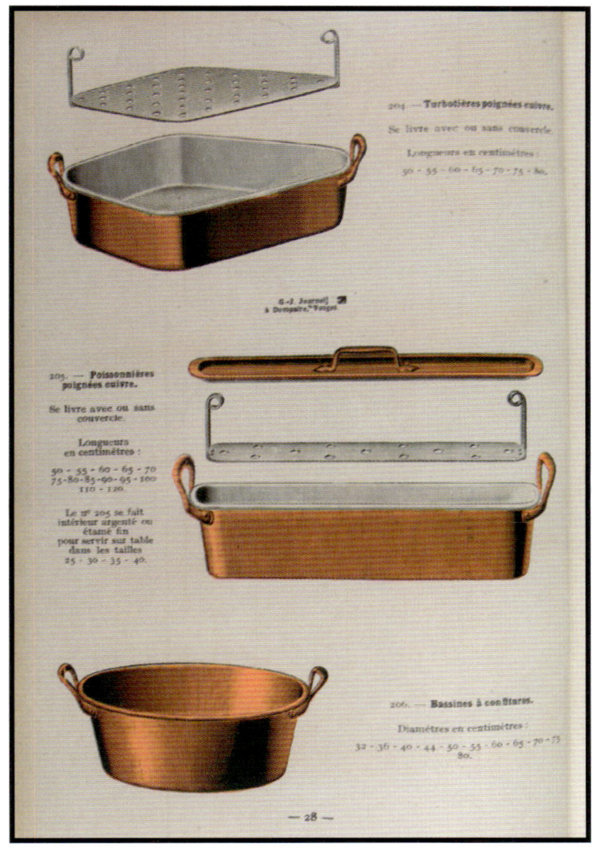

204. — **Turbotières poignées cuivre.**

Se livre avec ou sans couvercle.

Longueurs en centimètres :
50 - 55 - 60 - 65 - 70 - 75 - 80.

G.-J. Journel
à Dompaire, Vosges

205. — **Poissonnières poignées cuivre.**

Se livre avec ou sans couvercle.

Longueurs en centimètres :
50 - 55 - 60 - 65 - 70
75 - 80 - 85 - 90 - 95 - 100
110 - 120.

Le nº 205 se fait intérieur argenté ou étamé fin pour servir sur table dans les tailles 25 - 30 - 35 - 40.

206. — **Bassines à confitures.**

Diamètres en centimètres :
32 - 36 - 40 - 44 - 50 - 55 - 60 - 65 - 70 - 75
80.

— 28 —

184. — **Sauteuse évasée.**
Diamètres en centimètres :
14 - 16 - 18 - 20 - 22 - 24 - 26 - 28 - 30 - 32
34 - 36.

185. — **Plat à sauter,** 2 poignées cuivre.
Diamètres en centimètres :
18 - 20 - 22 - 24 - 26 - 28 - 30 - 32 - 34 - 36 - 38
40 - 42 - 44 - 45 - 46 - 48 - 50.
Le nº 185 se livre sur demande avec couvercle sauteuse.

G.-J. Journel
à Dompaire, Vosges.

186. — **Plat à sauter,** queue fer.
Diamètres en centimètres :
18 - 20 - 22 - 24 - 26 - 28 - 30 - 32 - 34 - 36 - 38
40 - 42 - 44 - 45 - 46 - 48 - 50.

187. — **Plat à sauter** avec couvercle sauteuse.
Diamètres en centimètres :
18 - 20 - 22 - 24 - 26 - 28 - 30 - 32 - 34 - 36 - 38
40 - 42 - 44 - 46 - 48 - 50.
Le nº 187 est un peu plus haut que le nº 185.

188. - **Braisière rectangulaire,** couvercle sauteuse.
Longueurs en centimètres :
24 - 26 - 28 - 30 - 32 - 34 - 36 - 38 - 40 - 42 - 44
46 - 48 - 50 - 55 - 60.

189. — **Braisière ronde,** couvercle sauteuse.
Diamètres en centimètres :
20 - 22 - 24 - 26 - 28 - 30 - 32 - 34 - 36 - 38 - 40
42 - 44 - 46 - 48 - 50 - 52 - 54.

190. — **Daubière ovale.**
Longueurs en centimètres :
30 - 32 - 34 - 36 - 38 - 40 - 42 - 44 - 46 - 48
50 - 55 - 60.
Le nº 190 se fait intérieur argenté ou étamé fin pour servir sur table dans les tailles
16 - 18 - 20 - 22 - 24 - 26 - 28.

191. — **Bassine à ragoût.**
Diamètres en centimètres :
18 - 20 - 22 - 24 - 26 - 28 - 30 - 32 - 34 - 36 - 38
40 - 45 - 50 - 55 - 60.
Le nº 191 se fait intérieur argenté ou étamé fin pour servir sur table dans les tailles
12 - 14 - 16 - 18 - 20 - 22 - 24.

— 25 —

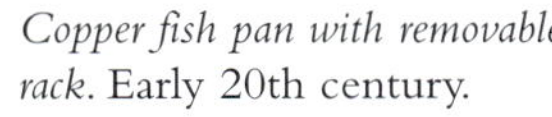

Copper fish pan with removable rack. Early 20th century.

Copper game pan. Early 20th century.

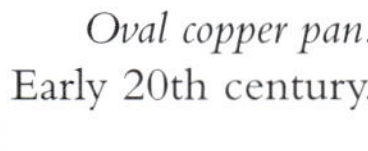

Oval copper pan. Early 20th century.

Wrought iron grill with pivoting rack. Early 20th century.

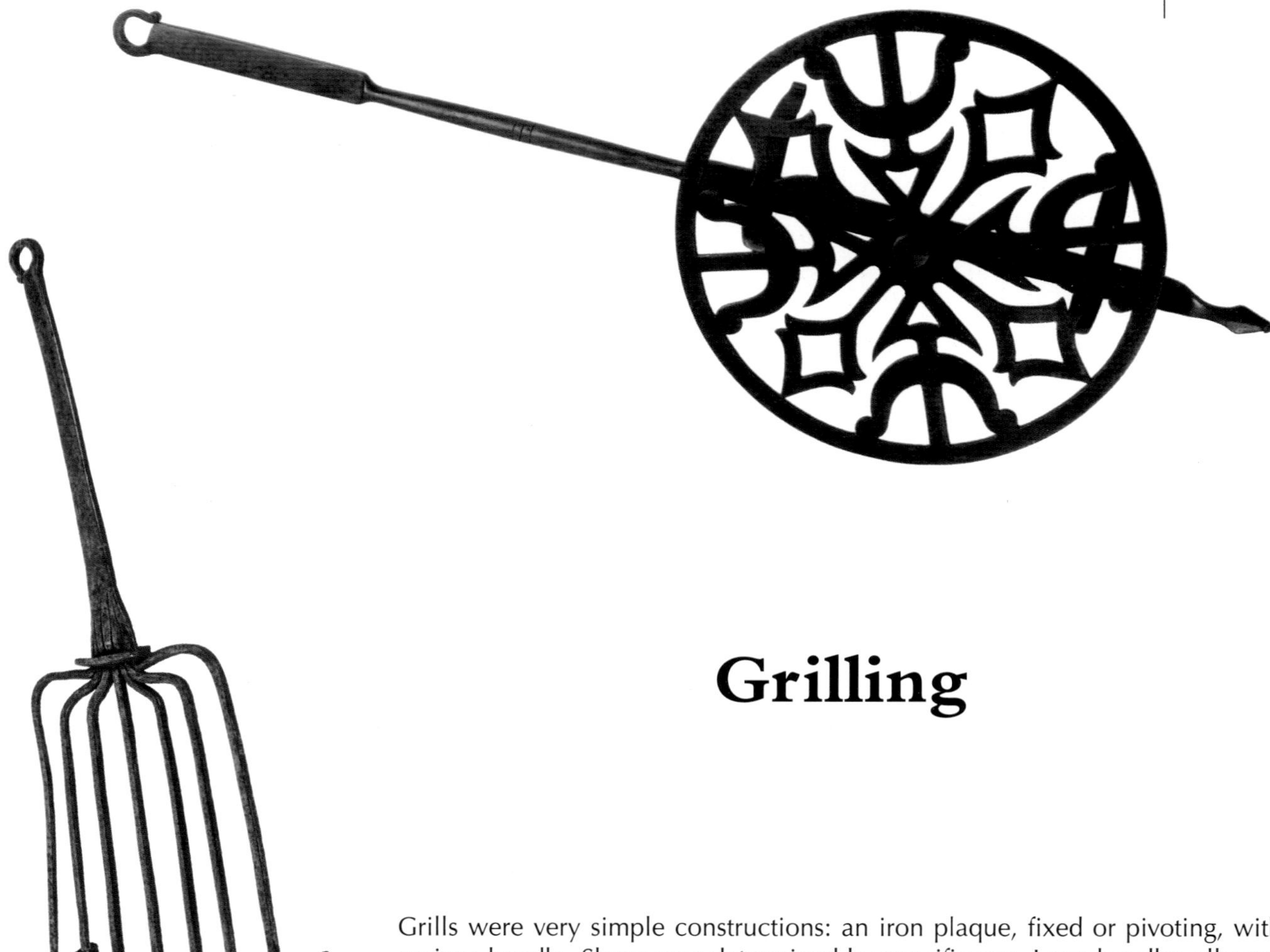

Grilling

Three-footed wrought iron tripod meat grill. 19th century.

Grills were very simple constructions: an iron plaque, fixed or pivoting, with an iron handle. Shape was determined by specific use. Long handles allowed them to be used more safely; wooden grips, a more recent innovation, gave added protection for hands.

Grills were used to broil meat, sausage, apples, bread, or to melt cheese. Some models were decorated with delicate openwork, while others were a simple series of straight or curved iron bars.

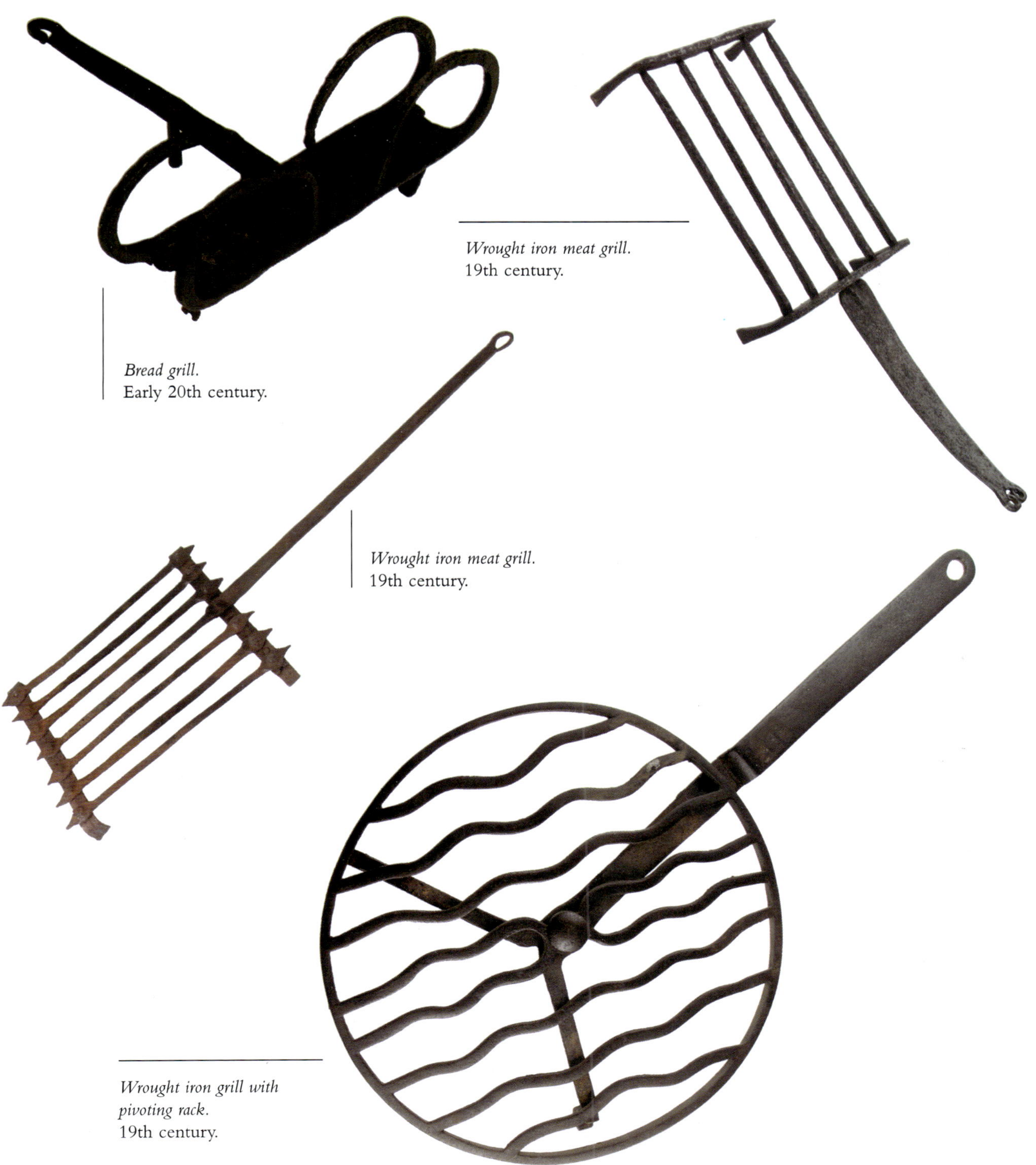

Bread grill.
Early 20th century.

Wrought iron meat grill.
19th century.

Wrought iron meat grill.
19th century.

Wrought iron grill with pivoting rack.
19th century.

Beignet irons.
Early 20th century.

Frying

Until the middle of the 15th century, bakers sold bread as well as pastries. From that time on, the latter became the monopoly of *pâtissiers*, pastry cooks, who had formerly prepared and sold meat and fish *pâtés*. Almond pastries, macaroons and frangipane were popular specialities in the late Middle Ages. In the 16th century, convents sold cake-like pastries and *beignets* to support their charities.

These doughnut-like sweet cakes were made with beignet irons: they were first heated, then plunged in the batter and then in hot oil. What makes these utensils interesting is their shape. Craftsmen drew on popular folk art designs such as stars, flowers, hearts, and fleur-de-lys to decorate the heads of the irons.

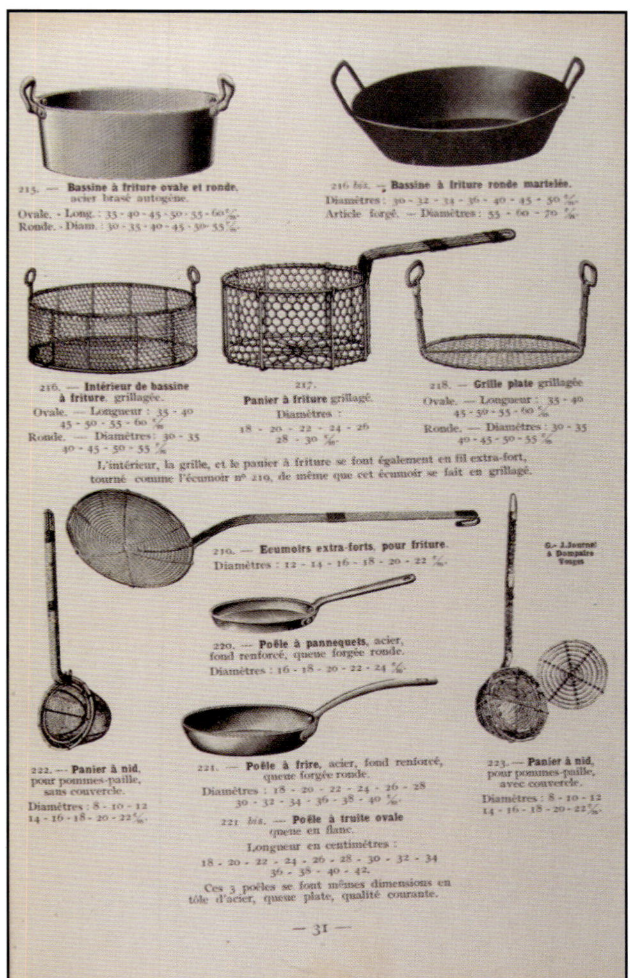

215. — **Bassine à friture ovale et ronde**, acier brasé autogène.
Ovale. - Long. : 35 - 40 - 45 - 50 - 55 - 60 %.
Ronde. - Diam. : 30 - 35 - 40 - 45 - 50 - 55 %.

216 *bis*. — **Bassine à friture ronde martelée.**
Diamètres : 30 - 32 - 34 - 36 - 40 - 45 - 50 %.
Article forgé. — Diamètres : 55 - 60 - 70 %.

216. — **Intérieur de bassine à friture**, grillagée.
Ovale. — Longueur : 35 - 40 45 - 50 - 55 - 60 %.
Ronde. — Diamètres : 30 - 35 40 - 45 - 50 - 55 %.

217. **Panier à friture** grillagé.
Diamètres :
18 - 20 - 22 - 24 - 26 28 - 30 %.

218. — **Grille plate** grillagée
Ovale. — Longueur : 35 - 40 45 - 50 - 55 - 60 %.
Ronde. — Diamètres : 30 - 35 40 - 45 - 50 - 55 %.

L'intérieur, la grille, et le panier à friture se font également en fil extra-fort, tourné comme l'écumoir nº 219, de même que cet écumoir se fait en grillagé.

219. — **Ecumoirs extra-forts, pour friture.**
Diamètres : 12 - 14 - 16 - 18 - 20 - 22 %.

G.-J. Journel à Dompaire Vosges

220. — **Poêle à pannequets**, acier, fond renforcé, queue forgée ronde.
Diamètres : 16 - 18 - 20 - 22 - 24 %.

222. — **Panier à nid**, pour pommes-paille, sans couvercle.
Diamètres : 8 - 10 - 12 14 - 16 - 18 - 20 - 22 %.

221. — **Poêle à frire**, acier, fond renforcé, queue forgée ronde.
Diamètres : 18 - 20 - 22 - 24 - 26 - 28 30 - 32 - 34 - 36 - 38 - 40 %.

221 *bis*. — **Poêle à truite ovale** queue en flanc.
Longueur en centimètres :
18 - 20 - 22 - 24 - 26 - 28 - 30 - 32 - 34 36 - 38 - 40 - 42.
Ces 3 poêles se font mêmes dimensions en tôle d'acier, queue plate, qualité courante.

223. — **Panier à nid**, pour pommes-paille, avec couvercle.
Diamètres : 8 - 10 - 12 14 - 16 - 18 - 20 - 22 %.

— 31 —

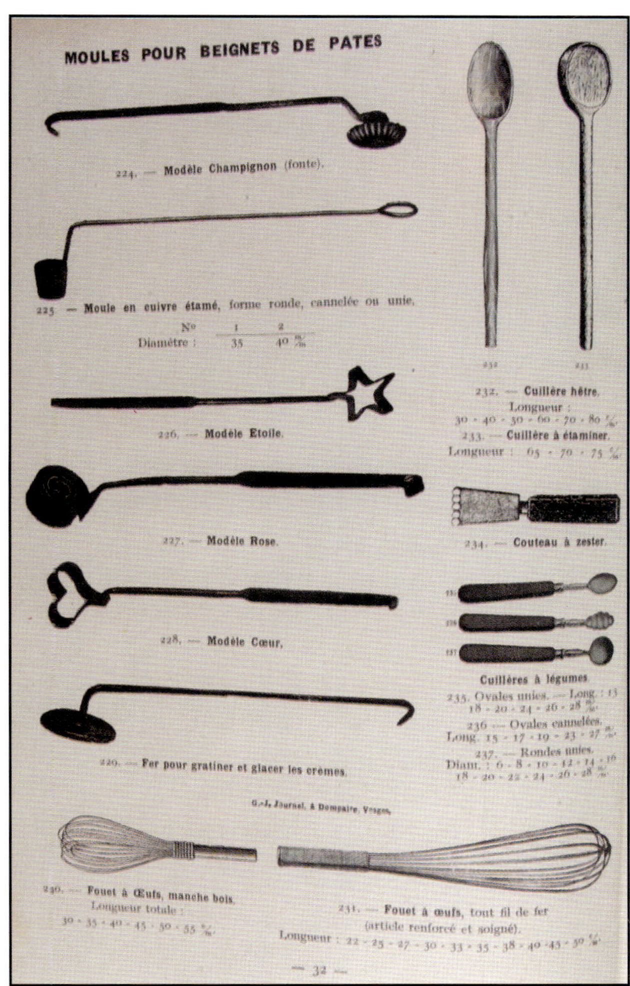

MOULES POUR BEIGNETS DE PATES

224. — **Modèle Champignon** (fonte).

225 — **Moule en cuivre étamé**, forme ronde, cannelée ou unie.

Nº	1	2
Diamètre :	35	40 %

226. — **Modèle Etoile.**

227. — **Modèle Rose.**

228. — **Modèle Cœur.**

229. — **Fer pour gratiner et glacer les crèmes.**

232. — **Cuillère hêtre.**
Longueur :
30 - 40 - 50 - 60 - 70 - 80 %.

233. — **Cuillère à étaminer.**
Longueur : 65 - 70 - 75 %.

234. — **Couteau à zester.**

Cuillères à légumes
235. Ovales unies. — Long. : 15 18 - 20 - 24 - 26 - 28 %.
236 — Ovales cannelées. Long. 15 - 17 - 19 - 23 - 27 %.
237. — Rondes unies. Diam. : 6 - 8 - 10 - 12 - 14 - 16 18 - 20 - 22 - 24 - 26 - 28 %.

G.-J. Journel, à Dompaire, Vosges.

230. — **Fouet à Œufs, manche bois.**
Longueur totale :
30 - 35 - 40 - 45 - 50 - 55 %.

231. — **Fouet à œufs**, tout fil de fer (article renforcé et soigné).
Longueur : 22 - 25 - 27 - 30 - 33 - 35 - 38 - 40 - 45 - 50 %.

— 32 —

Pages from *Catalogue de fournitures générales de cuisine,* G. J. Journel Co. Early 20th century.

Skimming ladle.
Early 20th century.

Wicker basket with wooden handle. 20th century. A metal wire adds reinforcement.

Rectangular wicker basket with wooden slat bottom. 20th century.

Transporting

Exemplified by its lightweight sturdiness, basketwork has always been essential to all phases of daily life. A multitude of objects exist from the past principally in woven willow or other plant fibers such as hazel, chestnut, straw or rattan. The closeness of the weave was adapted to the specific use of the basket.

In the Middle Ages, basket weavers and winnowers freely produced woven items until the profession was organized into trade guilds during the 15th century. Their activity continued until an edict in 1776 abolished their authority; basketry was then controlled by craftsmen-directed associations. It remained essentially in the hands of a multitude of small production units until the mid-19th century when the profession became industrialized. The number of products was phenomenal: woven articles were produced for fishing, agriculture, hunting, bread making, etc. Baskets of specific sizes served as units of measure for cider, apples or grapes. Others were used to carry eggs, oysters, cheese and sea salt; there were also dossers for grape harvesting, closed baskets for carrying poultry to the market, traps for fish and seafood...

Metal milk pot.
20th century.

Wooden grain measure.
Ariège, 19th century.
This was probably also used as a pail.

Glazed earthenware water bottle. Charentes, 19th century.

Metal bottle carrier.
20th century.

Water jug. Ariège, 19th century. The jug was carried on the head.

Hand-blown glass preserving jar.
Mildenstein, Alsace, 19th century.

Glass preserving jar.
20th century.

Glass preserving jar.
Early 20th century.

Preserving

Preserving food has always been a constant problem for mankind. Certain methods like sun-drying, smoking and curing were practised in Antiquity. Stoneware vessels of different sizes and shapes were produced for the storage of meat, fish and vegetables in salt or brine. This type of crockery resists the high acidity level of salt and vinegar-based preparations. Glass bottles and demijohns were better adapted to the storage of wine and alcohol because glass did not alter their taste. These were handblown until the 18th century and bear the mark of the cane on the punt of the bottle.

Glass jars and bottles were also commonly used for preserving fruits and vegetables, but if poorly closed, the contents of the containers quickly spoiled. In the early 19th century, the confectioner Nicolas Appert developed a technique for preserving food which permitted it to retain its qualities and apparent freshness. Bottles were filled with food before being carefully closed with wired lids and cooked in huge boilers. The heat killed bacteria and since the containers were vacuum-packed, the contents remained edible for longer periods of time. Less fragile tin cans progressively replaced glass containers.

Alcohol demijohn.
19th century.

Stoneware oil storage jar.
Beauvaisis, 18th century.

Partially-glazed storage jar.
19th century.

Porcelain olive oil pitcher with wooden lid. Provence, 19th century.

Stoneware salting jar and storage pot. Beauvaisis, 19th century.

Chromolithographed white metal tins. 20th century.

Metal tins

Metal tins include all sorts of white metal containers decorated with chromolithographs used for storing cookies, candies, chocolate and even sometimes preparations like mustard. Thomas Huntley, an English baker, is credited with the invention of hand-painted metal boxes decorated with stencils as packages for fragile sweets in the 1850's. The invention of chromolithography, a new printing technique, was rapidly used to decorate these tins: the first industrially-produced container decorated using this process was the *Ben George* of the Huntley and Palmer Biscuit Company. In France, large companies such as Lefèvre-Utile (LU), Geslot-Voreux, Galettes Saint-Michel, as well as Olibet also presented their products in similarly decorated tins.

From a collector's point of view, the Golden Age of boxes in sheet metal dates from the late 19th century until the 1920's.

Chromolithographed white metal tins. 20th century.

Above: *Wooden salt box.* Early 20th century.
Right: *Porcelain salt box with wooden lid.* 20th century.

Enamelled salt boxes with wooden or metal lids. 20th century.

Enamelled canister sets.
20th century.

Copper molds.
Napoleon III period.

Decorating

In times past, many pastries and cakes were baked in specific molds for specific preparations. This explains the production of so many models in so many different sizes. Sources of inspiration for their decoration came from the animal and plant worlds, from geometry and architecture, or were related to special events such as a baptism or a marriage.
Characteristic molds existed for the *Kouglof*, an Alsatian cake, as well as for *charlottes,* pound cakes, jellies and *madeleines.* There were heart, tree or animal-shaped molds; still others were in the shape of human figures.
Highly valued by collectors for their simple beauty, copper molds were used for cakes, chocolate, gingerbread and even waffles. The most basic models were cylindrical with a hole in the center for *charlottes.* It is always magical to see the form of the cake when it is unmolded.
In the beginning of the 19th century, tinsmiths began to produce molds in white metal, imitating traditional models in glazed earthenware. They were made in two interlocking halves for easy handling during unmolding. From 1820 on, leading manufacturers of culinary molds included Pinat, Cadot, Létang and later on, Sommet.

Copper molds.
Napoleon III period.

Copper chocolate mold. Early 20th century.

Articulated white metal chocolate molds. Early 20th century.

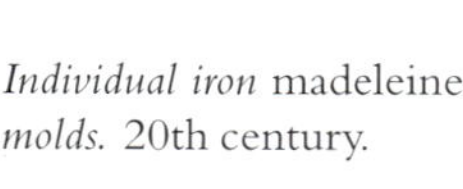

Individual iron madeleine *molds.* 20th century.

Glazed earthenware mold representing Hansel and Gretel. Soufflenheim, Alsace, 19th century.

Heart-shaped glazed earthenware cake mold. Alsace, 19th century.

Glazed earthenware cake mold. Soufflenheim, Alsace, 19th century.

Glazed earthenware Kugelhof cake molds. Soufflenheim, 19th century.

Carved wood bread stamp,
19th century.

Carved wood bread stamp,
19th century.

Carved wood butter stamp. 19th century.

Bread and butter stamps

Wood was often utilized by households to make decorative culinary utensils. During the long winters, especially in mountainous regions, peasants found the time to carve these useful objects. They borrowed from a large repertoire of folk art motifs, often adding personal inscriptions to the decoration of small chests and caskets, bread stamps, as well as butter stamps and rolls.

In rural areas until the end of the 19th century, bread dough was prepared at home and then cooked in the communal village oven. Each household needed a distinctive stamp to identify its baked goods. Blocks of butter were marked in like manner, so that customers could recognize producers easily at the market.

These stamps were hand-carved in boxwood, walnut or resinous wood and could take various geometrical shapes: ovoid, conical, spherical. Sometimes, the craftsman added his motto or a date of personal importance. It was an interesting manner of signing one's work.

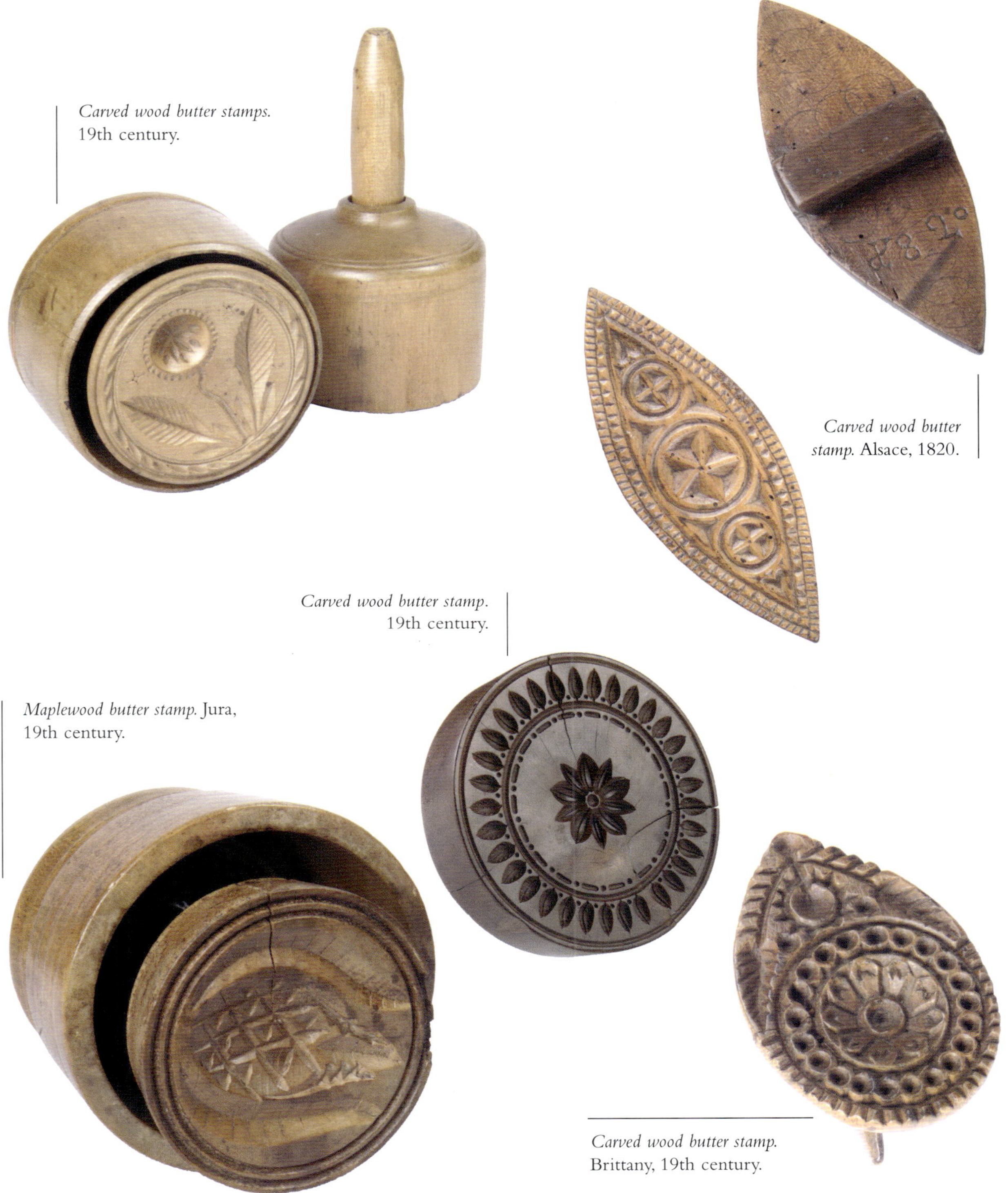

Carved wood butter stamps. 19th century.

Carved wood butter stamp. Alsace, 1820.

Carved wood butter stamp. 19th century.

Maplewood butter stamp. Jura, 19th century.

Carved wood butter stamp. Brittany, 19th century.

Carved wood butter plaque. 19th century.

Carved wood butter rolling pin stamps. 19th century.

Articulated butter mold.
19th century.

Articulated butter mold.
19th century.

Carved wood butter rolling pin stamp. 19th century.

Articulated butter mold.
19th century.

Glazed earthenware soup tureen.
20th century.

Glazed earthenware soup tureen. 20th century.

Copper ladles.
19th century.

Serving

The first direct mention of soup tureens dates from 1782, in an article in the *Annonce du Journal* de France where a tureen is included in the list of a Royal Sèvres porcelain service commissioned by Louis XVI. Throughout the 19th century, soup tureens were part of standard household tableware. Round, oval, rectangular or polygonal in generous proportions, they were traditionally produced in earthenware, porcelain or metal. Although many have a central base, others are footed. Some feature a matching platter or stand.

Wooden ladles. 20th century.

Glazed earthenware soup tureen with low relief decoration. 20th century.

Folding iron ladle. 18th century.

Glazed earthenware soup tureen. 20th century.

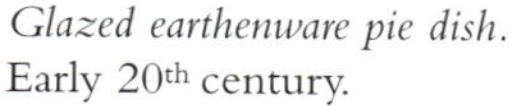

Glazed earthenware pie dish.
Early 20th century.

Scalloped-edged glazed earthenware dish. 19th century.

Flat dishes and platters were produced in different materials - especially metal, porcelain, or pottery - and in different shapes - rectangular, square, or polygonal. Those in glazed earthenware were often round. Some were completely flat with raised edges like pie tins, while others resembled soup plates and had a larger capacity. They were mainly used to present a wide variety of foods.
The patterns used to decorate them were often based on the circle, or quite simply a series of concentric circles or spirals. The center of the dish was often the point of departure for symmetrical or repetitive motifs. Although these are highly decorative objects, the numerous knife marks cutting through the glaze are proof of their regular use.

Glazed earthenware tart dish. Soufflenheim, Alsace, 19th century.

Glazed earthenware dishes. 19th century.

Glazed earthenware dishes. Martincamp, Haute-Normandie, 19th century.

Glazed earthenware dishes.
Soufflenheim, Alsace,
19th century.

Alsatian pottery

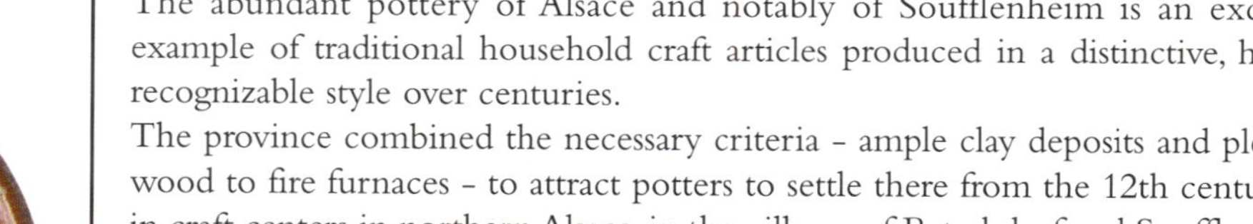

The abundant pottery of Alsace and notably of Soufflenheim is an excellent example of traditional household craft articles produced in a distinctive, highly-recognizable style over centuries.
The province combined the necessary criteria - ample clay deposits and plentiful wood to fire furnaces - to attract potters to settle there from the 12th century on in craft centers in northern Alsace, in the villages of Betschdorf and Soufflenheim. The production of glazed earthenware with its pure lines and attractive designs developed from the 15th century on and continued to flourish until the middle of the 19th century. Multitudes of jugs, dishes, cake molds and casserole dishes were decorated with characteristic red, white or green floral designs on black, red or ocre backgrounds. Simple daisy-like floral or foliated scroll motifs predominated. Low-relief decoration was also typical of Alsatian pottery.

Glazed earthenware dishes.
19th and 20th century.

Wicker basket.
Late 19th century.

Wicker basket.
18th century.

Presenting

Most baskets were extremely utilitarian and served as packaging for transporting foodstuffs. Some, however, were more ornamental. Equipped with only light decorative handles, many open baskets were intended to be placed in the middle of the kitchen table or on a sideboard. Filled with fruit, vegetables or eggs, they added a touch of color to the kitchen. These evolving still lifes were regularly added to and subtracted from, depending on culinary needs.

Wicker kitchen baskets.
20th century.

Coloured wicker basket.
Charles X period.

Egg baskets

In the 18th century, trompe-l'œil objects were quite fashionable and many pottery studios produced casserole dishes and soup tureens in the shape of rabbits, pheasants or roosters. In the second half of the 19th century and the early 20th century, trompe-l'œil hens brooded on baskets. They were produced in faience, bisque or sometimes in opaline. Eggs could be stored inside or presented on removable stands. Production centers in France included Nevers and Rouen. The hens were decorated in bright colors as were the trompe-l'œil woven baskets.

Twisted wire egg holder.
First half of the 20th century.

Faience egg baskets.
mid 19th century.

Faience egg baskets.
mid 19th century.

Uncorking

Wrought iron and steel corkscrew with mechanism. 1905.

Wrought iron and steel corkscrew with mechanism. Late 19th century.

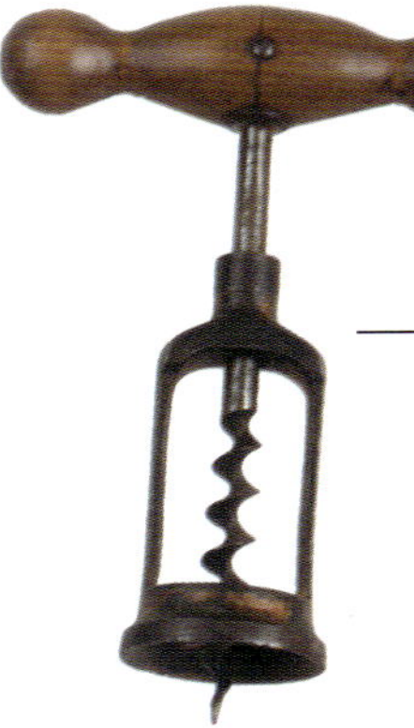

Wrought iron corkscrew with mechanism. Late 19th century.

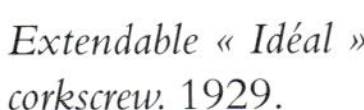

Extendable « Idéal » corkscrew. 1929.

The corkscrew was a 17th century invention. Until then, wine had been stored in wooden casks. When vintners started storing it in glass bottles, a tightly fitted piece of cork was used as a stopper. A tool was needed to extract the cork. The shape and size of the corkscrew handle were subject to careful study as was its decoration; however ornate it might be, the user had to be able to grip it firmly in his hand. During the 17th century, manufacturers let their imagination run wild: corkscrews were heart-shaped, or had revolvers, whistles or bunches of grapes for handles.

Since some Frenchmen never liked to be without a corkscrew, there were numerous folding pocket models. Companies used them as promotional items. Some models were equipped with small brushes to dust off labels.

Although there were literally hundreds if not thousands of industrially-produced models manufactured throughout Europe and the United States during the 19th and 20th centuries, collectors are able to identify their pieces thanks to their many particularities, including the shape of the bit and other patented mechanisms.

Wrought iron corkscrew with mechanism. 19th century.

Iron corkscrew with wooden handle. 1905.

Promotional wrought iron and aluminium corkscrew. Early 20th century.

Wrought iron corkscrew with a wooden handle. Late 19th century.

Wrought iron corkscrew with horn handle. Late 19th century.

Iron corkscrew with staghorn handle. 1900.

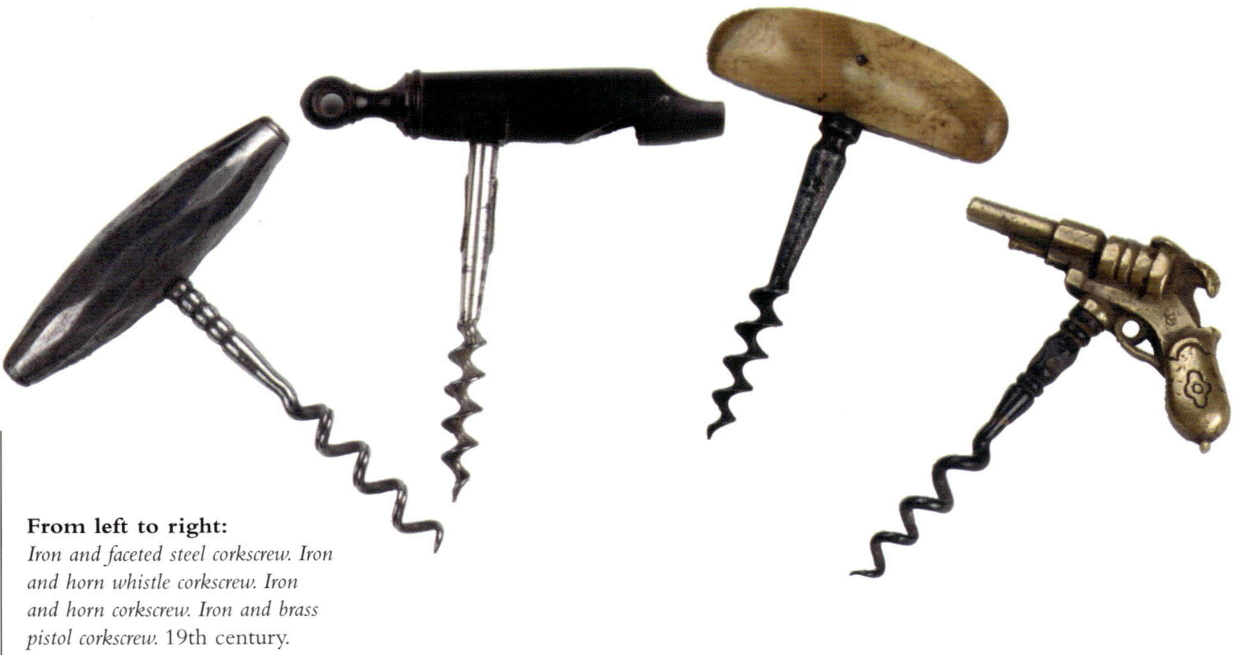

From left to right:
Iron and faceted steel corkscrew. Iron and horn whistle corkscrew. Iron and horn corkscrew. Iron and brass pistol corkscrew. 19th century.

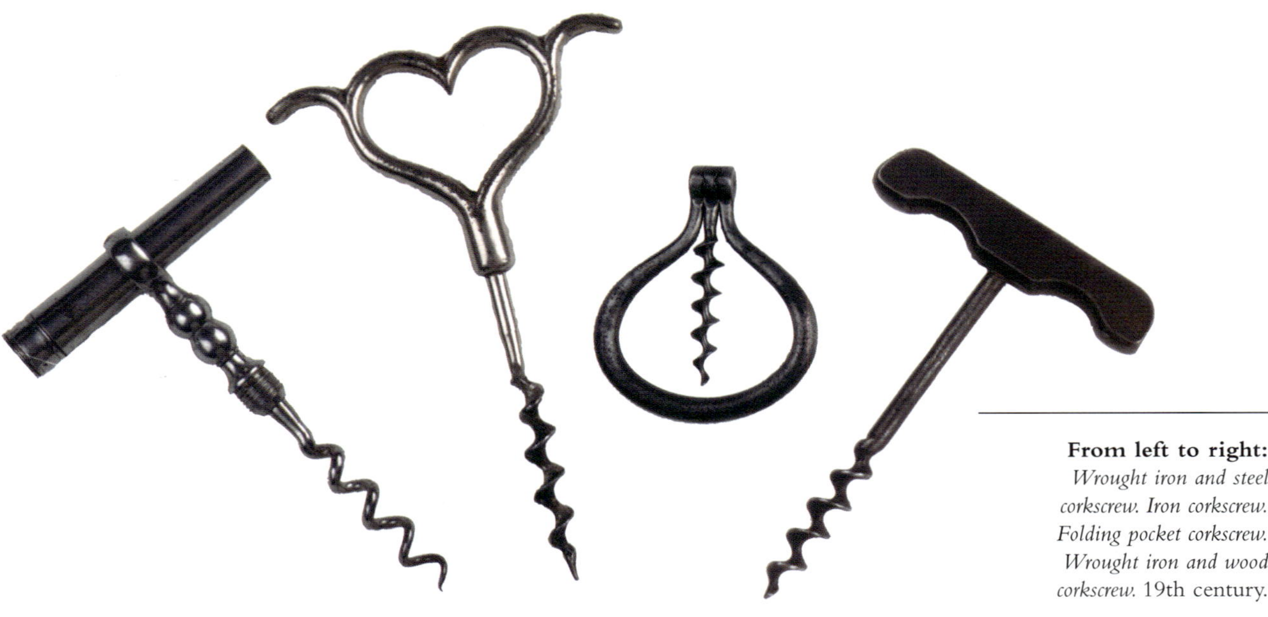

From left to right:
Wrought iron and steel corkscrew. Iron corkscrew. Folding pocket corkscrew. Wrought iron and wood corkscrew. 19th century.

From left to right:
Wrought iron and steel corkscrew. 1876. *Iron corkscrew with rack mechanism.* Late 19th century. *Wrought iron and steell corkscrew.* 1876. *Wrought iron corkscrew.* Late 19th century.

From left to right:
Iron « Le Diamant » corkscrew. 1889.
Iron « Bodega » corkscrew. 1900.
Iron « Le Record » corkscrew with wooden handle. Late 19th century.
Iron « Le parfait » corkscrew. 1950.

Pouring

Glazed earthenware water jug. 19th century.

Glazed earthenware carafe. 20th century.

Salt-glazed earthenware cider pitcher. Martincamp, Haute-Normandie, 19th century.

Jugs and pitchers were commonplace household objects. Different forms corresponded to specific uses. Large capacity containers were used to transport liquids. Middle-sized multi-handled vessels with a side spout served as storage for oil and water in the kitchen. Although these were highly utilitarian containers, potters paid as much attention to their form and decoration as they did to more purely decorative items. The large rounded surfaces lended themselves well to plant-inspired or geometrical patterns against richly colored glazes. On some very striking pieces, the glaze was applied only to the top part of the container and left to dribble down the sides. The bottom was of unadorned fired clay.

Glazed earthenware water jug.
18th century.

Glazed earthenware water jugs.
19th century.

Glazed earthenware water jug.
Saône-et-Loire, 19th century.

Glazed earthenware water jugs. 19th century.

Glazed earthenware water jug.
20th century.

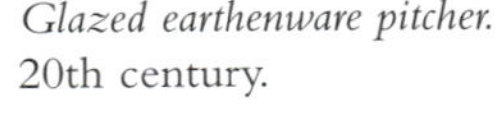

Glazed earthenware pitcher.
20th century.

Above and right:
Glazed earthenware jugs.
19th century.

Glazed earthenware jug.
19th century.

Left and above:
Glazed earthenware water or oil jugs. Saintonge, 19th century.

Marbled glaze earthenware pitchers. Late 19th century.

Glazed earthenware pitchers. Soufflenheim, Alsace, 19th century.

Glazed earthenware pitchers.
Early 20th century.

Oak and copper wine pitchers.
Burgundy. 19th century.

Left and above:
Copper pitchers.
19th century.

White metal coffee pot.
19th century.

Enamelled iron coffee pot.
First half of 20th century.

Coffee pots

Enamelled iron has been used for kitchen utensils since the 18th century. The industry, however, made great strides in the last quarter of the 19th century. These brightly colored coffee pots lined up on display in hardware store windows were always a delight to the eye. They added a bright note to kitchens as the smell of warm coffee pervaded the whole house. Easy upkeep gave enamel a significant advantage over copper and its sturdiness made it preferable to china.
Although all these coffee pots seemed very similar, there was actually a great range of shapes and sizes. Some were cylindrical, others were more spherical; some models were simple metal pots while others were coffee-makers with two separate compartments. Some had two or three-cup capacities, while enormous models held enough coffee for several days. The elegant curve of the handle enhanced the silhouette of more refined models.
Standard background colors - blue, pink and white - were also those of porcelain containers. Green and mauve were less frequently used, while bright red and yellow were favorites. Hand-painted or stencilled decorations made the pots distinctive. These are the main criteria for collectors. Floral designs such as bouquets of flowers were very prevalent. After World War II, enamelled coffee pots were replaced by stainless steel and tempered glass.

Enamelled iron coffee pots.
First half of 20th century.

Drinking

Glazed earthenware bowls with curved handles. 19th century.

Drinking bowls, like knives, were personal articles. In rural areas, they were used instead of glasses for drinking hot and cold beverages. They had a deep round shape and most reposed on a low base. Each region had one or several characteristic models and distinctive designs. Many bowls had small curved handles which fitted thumbs perfectly when the bowl was held in both hands.

In the 20th century, china bowls were produced industrially. They inevitably bring to mind breakfast. They were either decorated by hand or with stencils.

Glazed earthenware bowl with curved handles. 19th century.

Glazed earthenware bowl with flat handles. 19th century.

Speckled-glaze earthenware bowl. 19th century.

Glazed earthenware bowl with curved handles. Auvergne, 19th century.

Slip earthenware bowl with curved handles. Brittany, 18th century.

China bowls with stencil decoration. 20th century.

China bowls with stencil decoration. 20th century.

Draining

Copper skimming spoons and spatulas.
19th and 20th centuries.

Copper draining spatula for candied chestnuts.
19th century.

Utensils for draining fruits, vegetables and boiled meats are essential to separate solids from liquids. The simplest were spatulas or spoons drilled with holes in regular patterns.

Skimming spoons or ladles have been used by cooks for centuries. Copper was necessary for utensils coming into contact with acidic fruit, whereas white metal was preferable with dairy products. Some were equipped with protective wooden grips.

Different models of metal colanders were produced, some with long handles, others were footed and with side grasps. Enamelled metal was often utilized. Standard glazed earthenware plates and shallow dishes became excellent colanders once draining holes were added.

Copper colander. 19th century.

Enamelled colander with stencil decoration. 20th century.

Stainless steel colanders with wooden handles. 20th century.

Glazed earthenware dripping pan converted into a colander. Early 20th century.

Three-footed glazed earthenware colander. Early 20th century.

Glazed earthenware colanders. Early 20th century.

Glazed earthenware draining dishes.
Early 20th century.

Glazed earthenware spoon holder. Isère, late 19th century.

Organizing

Glazed earthenware spoon holder. Savoie, mid 19th century.

For centuries, our ancestors ate comfortably with their fingers or the point of a knife. Starting in the 16th century, forks and spoons began to appear at meals. In most cases, they were private possessions such as carved wooden spoons decorated with the owner's initials or other personal inscriptions. Knives also carried the owner's initials or other identifying marks. When the use of tableware became generalized and households owned numerous forks and spoons, these items had to be appropriately arranged.

Different solutions were adopted so that these utensils could be grouped together in an esthetic and practical manner. Those with hooks could be hung on a wooden rail of a sideboard or a buffet. Potters began to create specialized articles for storing knives, forks and spoons. They joined two or more cups to a rounded plaque. Holes were punched in the bottom of the cups so that wet utensils could be placed there to dry. Most of these spoon holders were hung on the wall.

These holders were soon produced in the different regions of France, each adding its distinctive decorative elements. In the Puisaye and the Berry, stands were made in stoneware whereas models produced in the Apt and the Castellet regions were in china. Potters in most regions, however, preferred working with glazed earthenware.

Glazed earthenware spoon holder. Vaucluse, 1897.

Glazed earthenware spoon holder. Ardèche, early 20th century.

Glazed earthenware spoon holder. Mid 19th century.

Glazed earthenware spoon holders.
19th and 20th centuries.

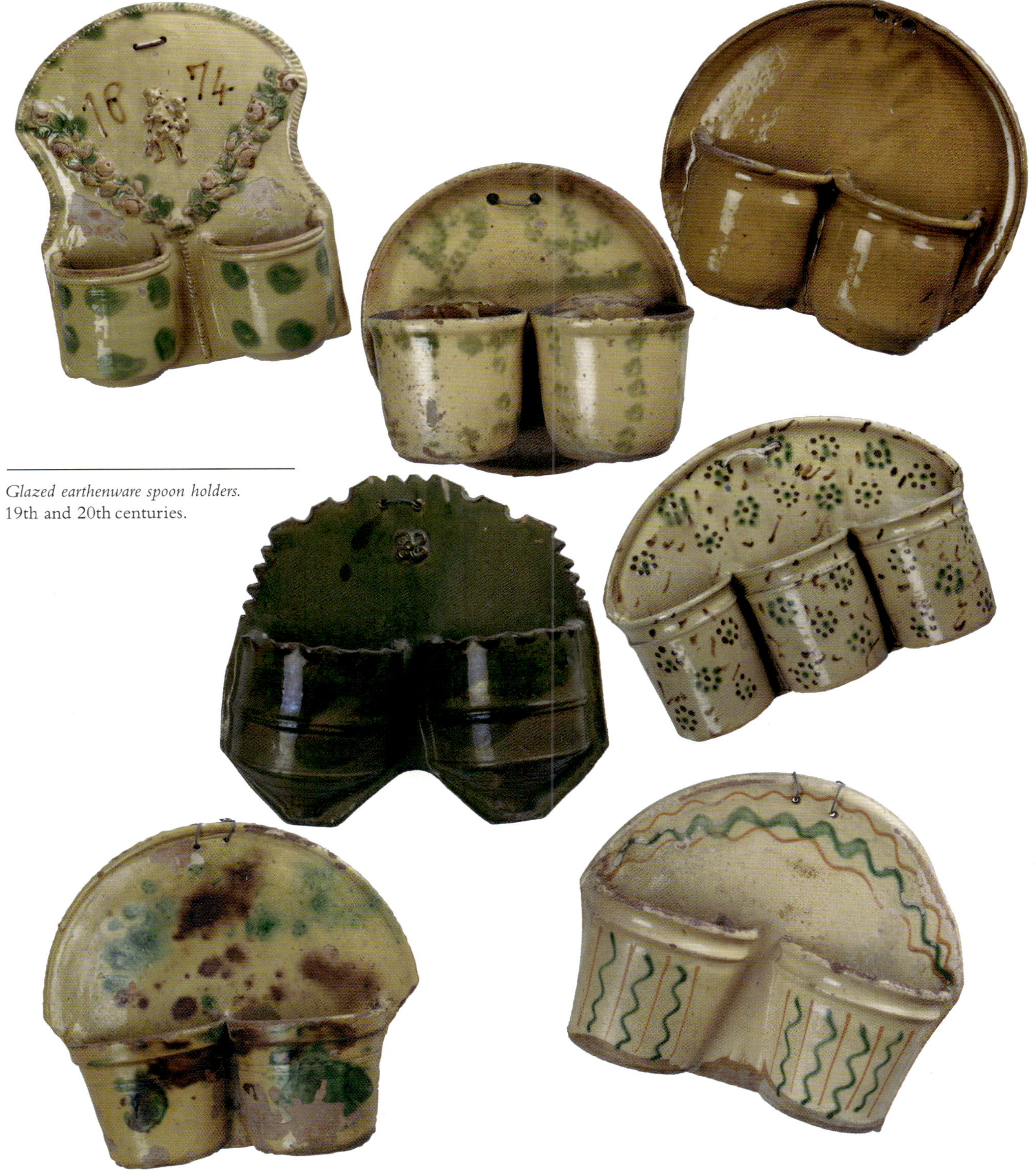

Glazed earthenware spoon holders.
19th and 20th centuries.

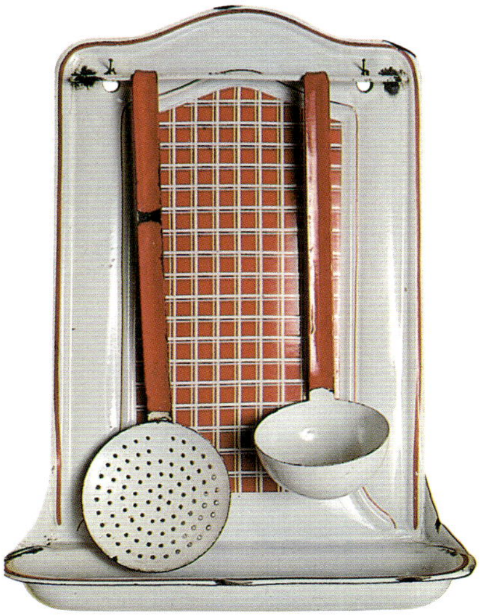

Enamelled ladle boards.
Early 20th century.

Ladle racks

Ladle racks are a 20th century version of spoon holders, often found in French kitchens between the 1920's and the 1950's. These brightly-colored, geometrically-patterned enamelled metal wall elements were based on a very simple principle: a bar was added to the top of a plaque which is curved up at the bottom. Slotted spoons, ladles, or other utensils were hung on the bar.

Unbleached linen towels.
20th century.

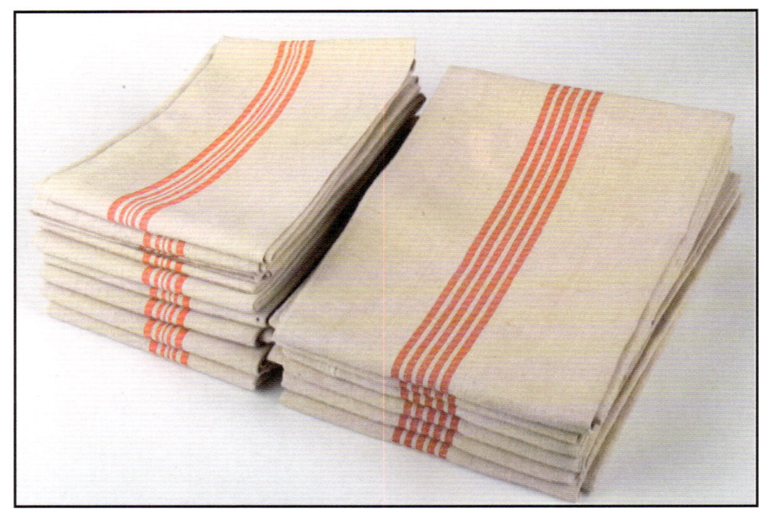

Wiping

Sturdy unbleached linen has a charm all its own. An important item in wedding trousseaus, towels first appeared in the 12th century, replacing the all-purpose linens used until that time as table cloths, napkins and wiping cloths. The first towels served not only as dish towels and dusting cloths, but also as floor cloths. Much time would pass before towels would be considered as part of pantry linens and used exclusively for kitchen use.

During the 19th century, the number and types of kitchen linens would multiply. There were specific towels for drinking glasses, porcelain, copper pots and pans, and still others for wiping fruit and vegetables. Brides-to-be prepared them by the dozens in their trousseaus along with other household linens. Many were embroidered in red with the families' initials, or simply edged in a contrasting color.

Absorbancy was of course the essential quality sought in towel material. Linen and hemp were highly sought-after fibers. Because of its higher cost, linen was reserved for the middle classes. Finely-woven cotton towels were perfect for wiping tableware. Coarsely-woven hemp towels were less expensive and used for drying kitchen utensils.

Bibliography

Crozes Daniel. *Ces objets qui nous habitent,* Paris, 1999.
Cuisenier Jean. *Les Arts populaires en France,* Paris, 1975.
Girard Sylvie. *Histoire des objets de cuisine et de gourmandise,* Paris, 1991.
Humbert Raymond. *Le Symbolisme dans l'Art populaire,* Paris, 1988.
Mouret Jean-Noël. *Les Cuisines de nos grands-mères,* Paris, 1995.
Lahaussois Christine et Pannequin Béatrice. *Terres vernissées; sources et tradition,* Paris, n.d.
Lecoq Raymond. *Les Objets de la vie domestique. Ustensiles en fer de la cuisine et du foyer, des origines au XIXe siècle,* n.l., 1979.

Catalogue
Objets civils domestiques. Inventaire général des monuments et des richesses artistiques de la France, Imprimerie Nationale, Paris, 1984.

We would like to thank the following people for their assistance in the realization of this book: Françoise-Anne Bachelier and François Bachelier for their generous sharing of time and knowledge, Raphaël Bedos, Hélène Breton, Marc Feldman, Bernard Masseloux, and Le Louvre des Antiquaires.

The objects presented in this book are part of the following collections:

Au Petit Bonheur la Chance
13, rue Saint-Paul
75004 Paris
Telephone: 01 42 74 36 38

Raphaël Bedos
41, quai de l'Horloge
75001 Paris
Telephone: 01 43 54 72 72

La Maison Bleue – Benoît Faÿ
3, ruelle Saint-Amant
60380 Gerberoy
Telephone: 03 44 82 45 76

Au Passe Partout – Marc Feldman
21, rue Saint-Paul
75004 Paris
Telephone: 01 42 72 94 94

Musée Rural des Arts Populaires
22, rue de Monceau
89110 Laduz
Telephone: 03 86 73 70 08

Marché aux puces de Saint-Ouen
Marché Paul Bert
93400 Saint-Ouen

Bachelier Antiquités
Allée 1 Stand 17
Telephone: 01 40 11 89 98

Michel Morin
Allée 1 Stand 20
Telephone: 01 40 11 19 10

Fatmir Taraj
Allée 1 Stand 19
Telephone: 06 14 38 15 87

Louvre des Antiquaires
2, place du Palais Royal
75001 Paris

La Galerie Pittoresque –
Dominique Martin
13, allée Desmalter
Telephone: 01 42 61 58 06

L'Herminette – Madame Leblic
6, allée Germain
Telephone: 01 42 61 57 81

Printed in Italy